Vellum

VELLUM

POEMS BY
Chelsea Woodard

ABLE MUSE PRESS

Able Muse Press

www.ablemusepress.com

Printed in the United States of America

Library of Congress Control Number: 2014944604

ISBN 978-1-927409-35-0 (paperback)
ISBN 978-1-927409-36-7 (digital)

Cover image: "Composition on wood – no title" by Emma Ferraro (Mef)
www.hellomef.org

Cover & book design by Alexander Pepple

Able Muse Press is an imprint of *Able Muse:* A Review of Poetry, Prose & Art—at www.ablemuse.com

Able Muse Press
467 Saratoga Avenue #602
San Jose, CA 95129

Acknowledgments

I am grateful to the editors of the following journals where many of these poems originally appeared, sometimes in earlier versions:

Best New Poets: "Finding the Porn Magazines."
Southwest Review: "Dinky Toys."
Measure: "The Illustrated Organism."
Blackbird: "St. Zita."
Birmingham Poetry Review: "Folk Tale," "'Self Portrait as the Allegory of Painting.'"
Poetry Northwest: "'Girl Worker at the Ponemah Mills.'"
32 Poems: "Prodigal," "Chaperone."

I am grateful to my family, particularly my parents, for being unconditional supporters. I would like to thank my wonderful poetry teachers, especially Corey Marks and Bruce Bond at the University of North Texas and Greg Williamson, Dave Smith, Mary Jo Salter and John Irwin at Johns Hopkins. I am thankful to Jordan Smith and Mikhail Iossel, who first encouraged my writing at Union College, and to B.H. Fairchild for his generosity and insight on this manuscript. I owe thanks to the Summer Literary Seminars and the Sewanee Writers' Conference for their support, to Claudia Emerson for her feedback on my work at Sewanee, and to Alex Pepple for his meticulous editing of this collection. I am indebted to Walter Hatke for his guidance in visual arts over the years, as well as to many classmates and friends, Tori Sharpe in particular. Lastly, thank you to Pete, who always keeps me entertained, truthful, and rooted in the world.

Every once in a while, someone will ask me what I think is essential to writing a good poem. There was a time I might have answered that I thought it necessary to have a good subject, an image, or a metaphor as a starting place. These days, I say that I, for one, need an honest emotion—an honest emotion I have some control over, but to which I am still vulnerable.

If I am right at all in this assertion, that an honest emotion is necessary for me and perhaps for a few other poets, then Chelsea Woodard is far ahead of me in her artistic maturity. *Vellum* is a stunning first book—a remarkable book no matter its number in what will be her opus—and part of its beauty lies in its emotional honesty, its unambiguous willingness to question, to linger over the things that matter to this poet.

In addition to her emotional maturity, part of what makes these poems memorable is Woodard's obvious mastery of language, her flawless sentences, the surprising way those sentences function and "mean" within the lines, the lines within the forms. Poetry is older than history, after all, and Woodard knows that she invokes and participates in a long memory when she writes in form. I am not the first to suggest that form in poetry is a kind of architecture, the varying structures known to many and bringing with them undeniable connotations that become part of a poem's meaning. *Vellum*'s poems have made me see that form can also be a kind of archeology, the way Woodard digs carefully down through the forms at the same time she is ever looking up and out. Seamus Heaney said on the subject of form: "I rhyme . . . to see myself, to set the darkness echoing," and Woodard's poems would also suggest that part of writing in form is to remind ourselves that whatever the history of the genre, we are writing from the physical: that those rhymes, those measures, are indeed "echoes"—real, heard, and of great comfort—and not learned technique alone.

Her subjects range from the ephemeral—mushroom hunting, figure drawing—to contemplations of what we can believe to be a lasting past, and also the slippage in that belief: a visit to Pompeii, for example, "dug out of its early shroud" to become a "bustling mausoleum." Woodard's eye can be backward looking; she is clearly interested in myth and mythmaking—keenly aware that "the rush of history blows coldly past." But she is not writing *to* the past; she is ultimately "faithful to the image shaping on the page," the page she creates in a real time and space, similar to the image she might create in the drawing studio, her responsibility there to the living models, "to draft the sudden passage of their bodies."

Her poems are faithful also to the natural world, her eyes attuned to its science and, as important, its mystery:

> . . . the work
>
> > of miracles—surely a miracle the way
> > > the hawk moth rustles from a sleep,
> >
> > a sudden winter, bitter, unforeseen,
> > > and flutters hungrily over
> >
> > the knotted snowdrops and the mud-wrecked plots,
> > > trailing the evanescent light.

While I obviously admire Woodard's formal elegance and her keen intelligence, those are often not enough of an alchemy to result in memorable and lasting poems. The parts of her art that are "heart-learned"—her curiosity and her vulnerability to the world and to the art—are what ultimately distinguish this work and give it its unique beauty.

In an era when so much mediocre verse passes for excellent, and when so much literary careerism obscures young poets who write their hearts out while maintaining a measure of humility, Chelsea Woodard's poems strike me as particularly necessary, and I am delighted and honored to introduce *Vellum* to you.

—Claudia Emerson

Contents

Vellum

I

Finding the Porn Magazines

The way a twelve-year-old will hide her want
in coded notes and locked boxes, afraid
her brother or her friends might see her secret

parts, her awkwardly scrawled heart inscribed
to *Ben* or *Mike,* until she murders its proof
with a lit match, a broom—we stuffed

that January night deep into our jackets
before my father drove us home. The hallway back
is dim and narrow, and you must take care

not to slip on the wet newspapers slicked
to the floor, or the tossed produce crates, the stale-
beer and gum-wrapper sludge smearing the tile.

It was a general store, the owner a tenant
of my father's, and the three of us were at an age
able to wear t-shirts without bras, to prize

field sprints over flattery, to note only in private,
in dismay, the way our stubborn hips
jutted out and our still-flat chests stung

from a foul ball or flailed arm. The bathroom lurked
at the end of the hall, and the men outside talked
as we steered, snow-booted, back. I remember wanting

to *look,* to peek through cracked doors, to explore
dresser drawers, packed boxes in attics; lifting
my shirt just enough to catch the pink skin's

sharp perk before the porch door slammed.
The magazines had been shoved in a pile
of *Boston Globes,* and from under the Celtics'

big win stuck a bare thigh, a breast.
Who noticed it first? Which one of us
ruled we would steal? Black-shadow exposed,

anemone-like, we thought *I'll never
be like those*—and took one each, so we
would know. The diesel engine droned

home, glossy pages stuck to my skin.
Like a crush, burning, bares itself, would betray
me that spring in the schoolyard, we stooped

from the car, the magazines hot as ice
in our sweaters while the house leered
at us through the floodlight's beam. Our breath

froze, crystallized what for years we would choke
in our chests, in the dark cracks
and pockets of dreams. My bedroom glowed

lamp-light red, and when my father tells
me this month of the stash they found
at the back of the old store, I feel the plush,

rust-colored carpet pressed up
to my stomach, the hot, prickling rush
that I cannot confess, ashamed still, even now,

to hunch over the bare limbs of the girls
who'll admit themselves just as the butane catches,
and the flame warps their faces to blue, then ash.

Folk Tale

for Nonny Hogrogian

In the story, I remember a hungry young fox
    rendered in pastels. He has stolen
from a strict-mannered woman in town, his tail's been cut off, his lot
    cast to repay her: stomach still swollen

with her Guernsey cow's milk, his head hung
    as he trudges the sad route she has mapped
for him. In the story, I remember bright sun
    glaring, the fox hunched and tailless, his tongue lolling, lapping

at air, his shame-path dry and sorrowful.
    And reading, I knew the author had lived
in our house—rust-colored shutters, fall-
    wormed, rattling rose hips, frost, pewter-halled air.

And in the book, every page held a trade: a pail
    bartered for rare, lazuli beads, a brown-speckled egg
for milled grain, straw for the mule pulling
    the plow. And I knew that each time, the fox had begged

for their pity—a sack of clean down, a gold coin, a gift—
    and that he'd at last made it back, the cold pail
handle clenched in his teeth, milk sloshing the step
    of the stern woman's house. And I pictured the blood-matted tail

handed back to him, dragged over our slab-granite walk,
　　　smelled the freezing ground
swelling—stumbled with apples, damp now, half rotten—
　　　the author's fingers rust-smudged from the work,

mine smeared with the chalk dust we found
　　　decades later on baseboards and rimed sills of doors—
the fine powder set into skin, each tenuous history
　　　heart-learned, unwritten.

The Flower Press

It was the sort of thing given to little girls:
sturdy and small, round edged, wooden and light.
I stalked the pasture's rough and waist-high grass
for worthy specimens: the belle amid the mass,
the star shaming the clouds of slighter,
ordinary blooms. The asters curled

inside my sweat-damp palms, as if in sleep. Crushed
in the parlor's stifling heat, I pried
each shrinking petal back, and turned the screws.
But flowers bear no ugly bruise,
and even now fall from the brittle page, dried
prettily, plucked from the memory's hush.

Study

*Take note that, before going any farther, I will give you
the exact proportions of a man. Those of a woman, I will
disregard, for she does not have any set proportions.*
      −Cennino d'Andrea Cennini, *Il Libro dell' Arte*

The models we would draw were never men,
        though they were fat and thin,
gray haired, cellulite dimpled, tethered at first
        in faded robes they'd loose fast

as they stepped into pose. And to begin, I found
        it difficult to look—turning a blind
eye to drooping breasts, to the dark-triangle tufts
        exposed when one would shift

her weight or turn to the light. Training my gaze
        to measure heft and line, the rise
of the hip, the pelvis's slight tip to the shade
        of a wall, the flesh soon showed

itself as what each woman wore: their skulls
        sheathed in thin skin, the swell
of a grown child held in the stretch-
        marked thigh or lower belly. I sketched

the latent angles of their bones, their forms
        wrought unfamiliar as the arm
or age-pocked cheek of a stranger. Outside
        the studio, the morning light spread

finger-like over the elms, over
        the just-sprayed drawings and our hands
tired of charcoal, smudged, burdened
        to draft the sudden passage of their bodies.

House of the Vestals

Pompeii, 1999

Our guide is young herself, a woman
      well-schooled in antiquities, who scans

sarcophagi etched in a language
      few can read. Clad in sandals

and long skirt, her figure Roman
      amid the throngs of t-shirt-boasting

student crowds like ours, she sidles
      between the tourists, close to walls,

as one who calls this buried city
      home. Assembling us inside

the sun-exposed foundation, toppled
      by heat and rediscovered, dug

out of its early shroud, she says
      that if a virgin broke her vows—

betrayed her duties, lured a man—
      she would be ushered down

the steep and torchlit steps of a tomb
        readied for her and then sealed

in it alive. Wading through ruins,
        we note infants and mothers locked

in fast basalt cocoons, and trust
        the solemn girl who ferries us

across this bustling mausoleum,
        trying hard not to decipher

fragments she's exhumed—*in this spot,
        seven*—and to ignore the smoke

from the still-burning mountain
        we could climb but don't, that leans

over the words scrawled in our notebooks
        and those missing from the house

where in a sea of ash
        we settle on uncertain graves.

Tarot

A favorite aunt—eccentric, hippyish, skilled
in astrology, in asking us
the grown-up questions, ones we had hoped
somebody would but hadn't—helped
us spread the disc-shaped cards across
the cabin's plastic-covered table

while we thought of things we'd like to know.
I conjured boy names, crushes
I'd never spoken; my sister mouthed
important dates, places she'd kiss or smoke.
The three of us bent low above the flush
of illustrated signs. I drew the Two

of Swords, my sister picked the dark-rimmed Tower—
images set against cheap glossed geraniums,
the spray-cleaned tablecloth our mother
bought and changed each spring. Hovering
above life's mysteries, balling our gum,
now hour-old, flavorless, we scoured

each tantalizing clue: two lovers
pelvis deep in waves, Fortune's rickety wheel, a naked
squatting girl, archers launching quiversful of arrows
at the sky. Patient, translating every scene, each grim, flower-
edged plot, our aunt made no mistakes—
at each prophecy, my sister gasped, covered

her heart as if she didn't understand.
I chewed my lip, clenched my thighs around
my fists until every uncertainty was met: our futures
smoothed over the flattened petals,
my aunt shuffling each picture back, each found
thing jumbled and falling from her hands.

Dress-up

It was the chest my mother stocked
with heirloom scarves and mismatched gloves,
a tiny room I stole inside to lock

the childish out. My schoolgirl loves
were small and unadorned, and so I'd wrestle
nylon tights onto my thighs, and shove

my feet in too-tall heels, rapt in the hassle
of a bustier's lace or bracelet clasp,
my plain and boy-shaped frame tasseled

for once with possibility; no longer would I rasp
my shins on rough barn planks, or pray to look
like Katherine T., who made recital parents gasp

how beautiful she'll be! I willed the book
with wood nymph maids to come alive,
and placed my body in their dancing ring. I shook

away the image of the lone crow poising to dive
into their midst in greedy swoops, and how
the sudden shame of nakedness drove

each of them to hide. And yet, no voyeur prowled
our house, and nothing waited in the sky
but evening rain. The looming trees grow

closer now, and in the mirror's eye,
I see the dark bird circle and fall.
No more is dressing meant for play,

the childhood room cluttered with dolls
whose porcelain limbs glow small and white
against the cobwebs and the crowded walls.

But it is here that I still track her flight—
inside the dusty shelves and splintered frames,
the faded storybooks she wished would write

the printed figure of her proper name.
Adult, I search each still-undecorated page
to find the girl's true illustration, form

every made-up scene, each flimsy stage
and costume for a glimpse of her—stumbling
through piles of grown-ups' clothes, still awkward in her age.

Posture Class, 1962: Spine-Mapping

Shirtless, goose fleshed, tucked into the back room
    of the girls' day school, the students queue

in single file: knapsacks thrust in labeled cubbies,
    uniform cardigans hanging from pegs,

cold hands cupped modestly to cover budding
    chests, argyle-clad legs crossed, wobbling.

My mother is the first in line, waiting
    to have her spine drawn from behind the screen—

each curvature recorded—anxious for signs
    of wrecks on the horizon, her backbone bent

by what's to come. I want to see all that the teacher sees:
    the straight-backed woman, shadow-veiled, who charts

thin torsos stripped of their training bras, the girls
    trusting her stern, spectacled gaze to augur them.

What riddle lies behind the mesh-grid wall
    of all that was? What hand steadies and guides

hers as she plots their bodies' path, traces
    each as something skeletal,

ignoring breasts, pale muscled flesh—their faces
    cropped outside the frame, illegible.

Pegasus

Rushing from sun
      into the cool beckoning must
            of the town library, we rummaged

through the stacks to find the title. Hidden
      as we had left it last, half blocked
            by Galileo's *Systems,*

piled nautical charts, Copernicus—
      the small black hardcover. Closed in
            by walls of shiftable volumes

we would never read, I pressed
      my finger to the printed line—
            the steady characters that told

the story of an ordinary boy
      hauled skyward by the myth
            of pinion-lift and muscle, farther

from us with each page-bound word.

II

Craftsman

Into the thick of pine and poplar,
inside the tumbled granite plot
that was a cellar hole, you spotted

an old carcass once—badger or mink—
bones stained the color of sunk
leaves, the mandible intact, the scattered ranks

of teeth and vertebrae weighting
down reindeer moss, the flat, bright
caps of chanterelles. Boreal acolyte,

disciple as you were of some lost,
primitive art, you dug and harvested
all of it: ilium, femur and rib, clavicle, tarsus.

No more a pilgrim's wooded grave.
No more a wreck of caved-in
clapboard drowned in sheaves

of last year's needles. Grinding
the bones into an ivory mound
for gesso, working the porous grain

of rotted oak or fire-thawed apple panels,
you scaffolded your work on feral
scraps, their frames the mineral

smoothing the passage of your brush,
your figures' rose-tinged flesh
propped always on a bed of ash.

And still the loss was irreparable,
and so for years you scavenged scuttles full
of fallen limbs, then glazed with pitch enamel

all you wrought—images built
on whitetail antlers and the quills
of hawks—their keel and gristle finally set

into some deathless, disembodied flight.

Uterine Vellum

Never exposed to cold or light, to wind.
Not to be licked or scraped with a rough
laboring tongue or herding barb, the skin
weathers scudding instead, the deft prick of the quill tip.

Suckled by neither air nor mother, on its back
this calf carries the gestations of strangers:
unburdenings inked into words, to tattoos
read by fingertip, born flesh.

Degas's Nudes

New mother, friend, no longer free
of the one who clutches at your chest,
your side, whose fingers I see cling
to the lobe of your ear or lambswool collar,
whose eyes drink in, unblinking, this
display of women caught in shades
of disarray—the falling curls
yet to be brushed, stark buttocks—
here you move languidly among
the tilting heads of other visitors.
We've come to see the body re-devised.
A many-clustered, mumbling throng,
each of us pores up close over
the curling pastel strokes and darker
lines, a spinal column glowing white,
a girl's neck from which she has just swept
up her hair. And though the pictures reacquaint
the female form with the quotidian—
the brothel and the bath, personages
snatched by chance, from below, from behind—
still what I see in each is something volatile
and new, a private confidence
laid bare, a modesty we each refashion
with our gaze, finding a woman's
parts—your breasts, you said—
strange in the eyes of someone else.

St. Zita

Basilica de San Frediano, Lucca

for Mary Beth

You had to see her for yourself, you said,
and so I tagged along, a foreigner
to churches, nervously reverent
in every darkened apse, inside the rich,

velvet-thick must, buttress enclosed and bordered
on all sides with somber della Robbia blue
and gold-leaf-tinted rapture, visible trusses, each form
mortared in place and deathless, separate from time.

Trapped in a photograph, I can still see the rush
of poppy-dotted fields, light hovering
in slow, translucent globes, your blond hair
drawing stares, the train ride uncomfortable.

Girded for centuries by ramparts, largely untouched,
the city beckoned us, and when we ducked
into the nave—leaving behind the sun-baked courtyard,
the hunched, black-kerchiefed women shaking

their heads, clucking their disapproval
of our bare shoulders and cameras, open-toed shoes—
and shuffled breathlessly into the cool
of yet another dim side chapel, we found her

whole as they had said: her glass case sized
to fit a child, limbs sapphire-wrapped, her forehead
crowned with roses. *Incorruptible,* they call her,
and in April lift her out into the square

to let the faithful touch her hardened face
or hands, the young girls' arms brimming
with daffodils. Though in my memory, her body's
anchored to the dark back of the chapel

where we pored over her frame in disbelief,
traced with our fingertips the wooden angles
of her wrists, her cheeks. Like you, I lit a candle
as we left her small, cold chamber for a blur

of unwalled country and a lengthening chain
of strangers, unremarkable, their names
not mooring anywhere—the field light
and our spare, convent-like room, your face

a girl's still then, looking solemn from the window,
looking still out from the dull blue of the veil
I had you wear for that one portrait I saved,
gave to you last year for your wedding.

Unicorn

Captive of tapestries, stitched into wool and silk,
gilt-woven, held still in dim museum rooms, her withers
wooden fenced, hemmed in by spearpoint, hunted
for hours with dogs, frozen in long abandoned myths,
in every glimpse of deep violet-lipped woods
and in the prayers of tower-locked daughters,
the homesick throats of sons—she has eluded us.

Seeking her still, we haunt the cellar-dark exhibit halls
that trap her form—not horse or goat, threads loose and fraying,
dulled—her likeness rendered gentle, hooves raised
humbly to some noble lady whose trove's signed over
to my one desire. Somewhere, years shut inside
its velvet box, there is a face that gleams, a hand reaching to graze
the snowy flank or forelock, the fine tip of her horn.

Mappa Mundi

The road to you is long. It is awash
        in torn-up roots and breaker spray
and I can't see the meeting of my feet
        on rock, or where the hard-packed clay

dissolves every receding step. I take
        no compass and no globe, no chart,
years-worn and creased to softness in the cold
        breast pocket of a traveler's heart—

rather I trudge inside these distant rooms,
        where hyacinths flicker in rain,
and mullions quarter the neighbor's farm, the view
        beyond the rippling pane

warped green. This is the truth we bargained
        for: the isthmus path, the crags
and thistle patches drifters now must cross
        alone. Out there, my courage lags

and the light's gone out of the waves. Interiors
        are what I cleave to when the far shore
crackles, when the ice under my skate blades
        snaps, our childhood pond now four

years turned to field. No oar can scull the bottom
        muck, and the toads and catfish have cast off
for other marshes. Where the lane veers
        to the oaks, where the hush has too long housed

the rolled up scrolls passed to disuse, the sea chest
        closed—the wand of the illuminator
waits. Calligrapher whose golden nib
        is gone, trace in the shifting air

your finite characters. There is no whale-road
        but the wake of ships, a floating place
I've come too late to, traveler, finding you lost,
        the way impossible to trace.

Mushroom Hunter

When a girl takes to the woods, she does not check
for rain. She does not bring
     a map or field guide, nor does she truss her pack
with skin-sheathed knives. Her tongue

searches the ridges of her teeth and wants
     for something unfamiliar, a taste
that's more of undergrowth than field, plants
     dense of flesh, dew-wet,

easily lost in ferns and moss. She has
     no truffler's snout to nudge
at the roots of ash or apple, to whisker fungus
     from its toad-masked plot.

She only knows to look when leaves are larger
     than the ears of mice.
When a storm is just passed or a brush fire over—
     the air thickened and doused

with smoke—she prods the trunks of long-deserted
     orchards, digging the rare,
spore-wrinkled caps she yanks from sleep. Alert,
     she sets the edibles apart

from each death cap and sulfur tuft, the fairy cakes
        and pinkgills that keep the sickbeds full
of belly-clutching kids and tourists, soaked
        to the bone from rain. It is the fall

she's hankered for, and though she craves mouthfuls
        of morel cooked in butter, salt—
she doesn't eat. Seeking the wood's outermost
        reach, she tracks the molt

of hares and red tails, pinching each flight feather
        with care, glutting herself on all
their bodies slough off as they ready for
        the cold, the cellar spell.

The Illustrated Organism

for W.H.

I.

Two disciplines today will span the room
of hipsters, science geeks and goths in coats
and hats, hunching above their fishy specimens
to draw. Already they've dissected the lean
and part-cured bodies for their key: air bladder, gill
or adipose—but mind the heart, whose bloom
of blackish pigment bleeds and floats
beneath the pupil's crude, incessant lens.
Posing as whole, the loosened skin's green
envelope balloons, waiting its fill.

II.

To draw the dead, the masters said to use
the palette of the living, only to choose
a paler shade to wash the brow. It's colder
now inside this attic room; the model folds
her long white fingers on her chest
to slow her breath—that frail, tenuous guest.
It's harder than he thought—to make her torso
slump into the chaise, wrist graze the floor.
Sifting dust, light pools scarcely beyond
the subject's toes. The artist lifts his wand.

III.

The finished sketches line his office walls:
day lily, monarch, dove. Guilty as Audubon,
Professor studies these flat artifacts
for flaws, but finds none. Cataloguers claim
them all, and having archived every last
passed over limb and part, remember tracks
crisscrossing in the snow, no two the same.
The rush of history blows coldly past.
As soon as we translate what it recalls,
the day is still, the breath of every body gone.

Diapause

for J.S.

Where you are, there are no butterflies—
    the ocean warm, the blacktail's skirl

always three miles above your heart. You say the sun
    slowly forgets you now, ebbing

each morning with the tide—that it's grown cold
    and red—a dull burn at your back

as you count syllables and Medrol, hours
    you bite your lip and wince and wait.

At twenty-six, you say it is as if you have been *waiting*
    for death, the mourners holding

at the water's edge, the gulls that won't stop
    shrieking. Some days the scar

along your spine threatens to rip—
    its white and crooked line the work

of miracles—surely a miracle the way
    the hawk moth rustles from a sleep,

a sudden winter, bitter, unforeseen,
    and flutters hungrily over

the knotted snowdrops and the mud-wrecked plots,
    trailing the evanescent light.

III

Urania Practica

I. *Ephemeris*

The authors drew celestial forms with human
faces, crudely etched, and made a formula
to plot the true position of the sun.
Earthbound and dwarfed by mountains, storms—
imagine knowing only the sudden warmth
upon your skin, the godlike silence
as it shone, bright from the cloud bank, once.

Charting the birth of every moon and each eclipse
proved that light waited still, behind
the curtain's slip that, dark and wordless,
dimmed the day to night, hushing the wind's
crack in the trees, the restless mind.
Marking moonrise and set, we were appeased
to know her silver ghost still glowed at least,

beyond our sight. We constellated stars
and gave them heroes' names, considered
time as cold and sidereal and far—
our spyglass magnified to spot what hid
anonymous before, left off the grid.
A homesick ship could bind itself to one
fixed point, already mapped—a drifter's sun.

II. *Meridian*

A diagram could show it best: you arc
the tennis ball and follow with your eyes.
Revolving is your throw, our dog, the park,
a child's laughter as her father tries
to balance on a barrel, teeters, and lies
defeated in the grass. Wheeling around
our heads: the dragonflies, light darting sound.

This fall begins our apogee, and farther
from the root we bloom and scatter, toss
our questions to the rain-slicked road, and answer
only when we can. Crowning our loss,
the nimbus spins unseen and slow across
an empty sky. You say you hate to be apart.
I mark the calendar, wait for our lives to start.

Aubade

It's always three a.m. and still dark
when you nudge me, fretting and sleepless, wanting
to talk. And I am riveted and locked
nightmares away from you: all swamp
and Spanish moss, great gnarled trunks
straddling the path I never get across

in time. But in this post-witching-hour space,
time hesitates: one breath crushes me in
then yanks me back—your mouth pressed
to my ear—your voice crooning Van Morisson
off tune. And while I'm fumbling in dreams,
struggling half comatose towards you,

through dark pine woods to darker room,
you drag me out. Watching me strangling
in fat roots, gulch trapped, left to the house's damp, the night—
the window's face is pitch and motherless.
But when I finally wake, the day
is dry and bright. You've gone, and there is nothing

but an old train car's rattle shuttering the light.

Harpy

Was she a sudden gust, some raw, squall-blasted
body from the north, claws set, the young man's teeth
grinding in sleep? And he is dumb to the dark wings beating
the glass, feathers the weight of flour sacks,
alizarin-tinged down sprung from her breast
where she is bird, bird, black talons scratching
the cracked pane, her prospect hideous. Though in a patch
of blue, unsettled light, sunk in his makeshift nest

of tousled bedclothes, sheet-creased skin, he dreams
he's reaching for her face. And when the sun, flooding
the small room, uncovers him in bed, he tracks a streak of blood
across his chest, and when he twists, the torn flesh screams.
He could not say if it was dawn, or just the threshing of desire
that drove him, slumber-fledged, stumbling to find her.

Dormitory

for my grandfather

Sixty years afterwards, you tell me how you lived
     in the same chamber as Thoreau,
your head bent over physics books, your slow,
       Midwestern tongue naming

each property of movement, of falling. Asleep
     now with the *Times* open across
your lap, the story just half read, half buried with the lost
     concert hall chatter, bass thrum,

steady hands—memory riddles back: old glass
     shifting the clock's face, each elegy
a march your father conducted with his wand. Only
     there is no cornet now, no soloist

floodlit upon the stage. The race is done. Outside,
     lawn mowers rip and stutter, zoom
over the tender grass, and when you wake, the room
     has dematerialized: your strain

drowned out by the ghost-echo of the metronome
     you gave me when I used to play, its hammer
warning from the draped and mote-filled parlor
     if a man does not keep pace. . . . Drummer,

where have you ushered us, what is this quiet place?

Chaperone

You never thought you'd be back here again:
      the pink, powder-primp throb
of giggly blondes and bass, of seventeen,
      all strut and swagger in this strobe-

lit throng you barely peer into to check.
      It's curious to watch
now from the side: you're wearing modest black,
      lurch clumsily to catch

a football player's arm, as he's bound for the door
      out to the parking lot
where late night's bottled and sloshing on the floor
      of someone's pickup.

Pulses race and stop, your stomach tight under
      your date's damp touch,
remember curfews ducked, broken on thunder-
      stricken roads that couched

your alibi: power lines down, his tire
      flat, you lied while picturing
Tim Pritchard's back yard, your bustle snagging briars
      in one rushed kiss. The click

of inexperienced heels pacing the hall
      returns you here: no flowers
now, your corsage pinned and crumbling to a wall,
      you watch them chase the hours

on steel-rimmed trucks, your fingers crossed
      they make it home in time
to stop the hallway clock—grinding what's lost
      with each relentless chime.

Dinky Toys

After long years of hoarding dust
in metal boxes, put up and locked

beneath pink insulation smog,
hot boxed in our old loft's garage,

a father's stash lost or forgotten—
my mother and I dig them out,

clean them to glisten in the casement
where we're lining them in ranks:

gunner-clipped tanks and armored cars,
green jeeps faded in sun, field guns

stiff from disuse, two hay trucks—powder blue—
a double-decker bus. It's time

to sell them now, or so Web records
tell, the bids on eBay pressing

go go go, but still no foot
stomps the accelerator down.

Only the groaning chassis rust
and creaking wheels, some caking off

in chunks, ache for the greedy palms
of boys who steered them once, across

the mammoth, stocking-legged terrain
of beige-carpeted floors, boys

who would never dream that far-
approaching day when they would trade

their treasured cars over to girls
who'll barter them for petty cash,

keeping one token Esso van alone,
stock-still and gleaming on the shelf.

Old Flame

Ours was an iced-in cabin or your parents' house,
        roads we knew well as the cast
of snow that every winter held the storage sheds
        and gravestones from our view. You taught

me that a place means time: hours and seasons, years
        spent under blizzard-glare and copper
autumn—canopies that, like the leaves, shiver
        and shift, letting their absent figures

and the ghosts of bodies, yours and mine, float
        down and among the small town's list
of those born and remembered here. So it is here
        that I remember you: the pond

prisoned in ice, the backyard where your father planted
        balsam trees, your hands nimble
as his lifting dark branches from the heavy drifts
        that even now bury the imprints

of that first love—fumbling, shy, one winter where
        the fire crackled and spat with pitch,
and evergreens pressed at the windows, heedless of cold,
        rooted in frost, new limbs springing.

Watermarks

Who notices the backlog stacked inside
the study walls, the volumes left unread
or unreturned to some bright Sunday long ago,
old roses floating in a bowl, the buzz
of lawn mowers and hay dust drifting past
stone steps and tumbling walls, the four-post bed
flooded in sun, the narrow, shuttered halls
adjoining white-draped rooms we never see?

But every now and then, lace curtains blown,
the rose hips' rattle on the house conjures
its ghosts, framed for a second in the window
pane; a single page held so the light
forces its memory, unearthed in washed out
flourishes and lines, letters from you.

Orpheus

The name belonged to the parakeet my teacher
    kept in the upstairs boudoir
of her big, empty-eyed house on Mercer Street.
    A portrait painter, the woman who taught
me to pronounce the holes and crevices,
    lived there alone. Her windows faced the offices
above the middle school. Crossing the bunker
    dim of curtained rooms to the sink
we washed our brushes in, I'd see the canvases
    she hadn't finished yet—unsettling, the faces
only part drawn, one eye in eerie focus,
    no mouth, a palm flesh-like enough to touch
held by a wrist that crumbled as I watched.
    And the work was life sized, the subjects large
enough to step on their exquisite toes and climb
    the stairs. Each took her months, and by the time
she put the final highlights on the ink gloss
    of the pupils, the lower lip, polished
the satin hem's sheen, a crease in the sleeve, the patrons
    had already grown impatient, their parlors
itching for the shades of their own likenesses
    preserved. Some days after our lesson,
I was allowed to visit where the bird
    spent most of the daylight with his head
tucked to his breast, next to a luxurious pink-cushioned
    bed, the left side always unslept in. Roused
by the brush of feet, the latching lifting, he made the house

start with his trill—something bare in it, racked
with the missing that no voice can summon back.

Coppélia

The magician's room is dim, and there he tends
alone to hosts of wooden limbs that clack
and roll over the floor. Nearing the end
of middle age, he peddles cleverly back

in time to fashion youth: lacquering her cheeks
with rose, framing her face in yellow curls
and seating her to watch the meager weeks
wear out their shoes, scuff through the whirls

of winter-grim and cold no doll can know.
But when he goes to sleep, he dreams
she's come to life, and his desire, too, grows
life sized, and forms the heart of a girl. What seems

gains shape, and soon the villagers believe
that she is real. *Beauty is truth.*
The artisan ventures to live
in this illusion, needing only the proof

of her unchanging face. The balding man winds
up his handmade toy, sets her to wheel
across the dusky stage—into the light that binds
her to this world where he must age and she can't feel.

IV

Radiation

for Pete

Your father has brought the mold of his head
back from the hospital to show to us. Strange
on the table. Innocuous even with holes

for his eyes, his mouth, holes where the beams will score
through him. It is plastic, white. A fact
he can point you to—*next Tuesday, in that*—

a skull globe he might set in your palm like a ball
during evening pickup games, sun spokes throwing
glare in his eyes, earnest now, betting on you

when I go, he says, as if to somehow steer
his listing world towards yours, where a loss writes itself
on the clock, and the bodies can't fall for the force of their lightness.

Indian Summer

Shamed out of doors by sudden heat,
by light setting the afternoons
aflare, scorching the living room's
tall windows to the south, I quit

the house for the woods, for long, measureless
walks past oak leaves hanging face-level
on spider threads, past the fall-littered
pond the heron stalks, restless,

testing this final cusp before she goes.
But when the sun makes us retire at six,
the clock half lit, the walls electric-
bulbed, I see that something knows

time better: a trail of ladybugs,
scuttled through mullion cracks
and dried caulking, seek their last
rest of the year across our bay

windows and white walls. And why
fear grips me now, quickly and sure
as frost, I cannot say. In this house, our first
in our first autumn, our novice try

to make a stronghold nothing could take
has been trounced. So I clear
them from the room with a few sharp smears
of the dishcloth. And though I will later ask

a friend if they were real—their shells
orange and faded, tan, not red
as they appear in books—I sense
already what I've done. What I feel

is the snow coming, winter flexing
on the edge of lawn, our threshold breached,
the rooms all overrun. To keep
what is still fragile safe, I press

the harmless beetles with my thumbs.
And through this spell, the cold still comes:
suspended, dead set, as I crushed
each little warden of our luck.

Black Trumpets

They grow in August near the roots of trees,
slow and unseen, covered by dung or dead leaves,
their flared caps not black, rather the shade of ash
found days old in the grate. Unearthed at last,
withered and sick looking in the basket crooked
under my arm, their bodies cringe from light
as the foot of a mollusk shrinks from an eager tongue.

I'd waited months to question you, so when
the secret hummed just out of view, its line
distended, menacing, I wrenched it out
by the stem. And when the dirt clods fell, doubt
found us alone in the wood. I wanted truth,
I said, and the gluttonous, swift hunter drew
her instruments up from the dim and blew us open.

Autumnal

i.m. Peter Hutchins, Sr.

By now, the kids have left. By now,
the summer folks have hauled their moorings
out, their garish boats. The floor's
littered with baby toys, the towels
your daughter sprawled into a heap
her daughter giggled from, trying
to be invisible. But yours isn't a season
fit for hiding. When the dock's
frost-crusted pilings jut, you tether
them again, retying. The sky's
cold, furious blue still keeps
you tired and restless, and you wake
near dark each morning to the blitz
of hungry finches on the lawn,
the flower beds your mother raked,
with pine needles each fall,
while you worked ahead of her, scanning
the lake for straggling geese or rocks, for suntanned
boys stalled on the water, calling.

Feral Child

*A little girl, pale, with dark eyes, lifted a dirty blanket
above the broken glass and peered out, one neighbor
remembered. . . . Her cheeks seemed sunken; her eyes were
lost. . . . The authorities had discovered the rarest and
most pitiable of creatures: a feral child. The term is not a
diagnosis. It comes from historic accounts—some fictional,
some true—of children raised by animals and therefore
not exposed to human nurturing. Wolf boys and bird
girls, Tarzan, Mowgli from The Jungle Book.*

–Lane DeGregory, "The Girl in the Window,"
Tampa Bay Times

Forgotten utterly and cast
out from the human fields
of post-school practices and playgroups,
plastic-wrapped snacks packed to outlast
the drawn-out schoolgirl's day,
this chanced-on creature flinches, shields

her black, retreating eyes with the palm
of her hand. Her nails are long,
clawlike and caked with months of grime,
but her skin is white. Stoical, calm
as the orphan in the silent film who mimes
the common history of wrong

miring her, when she drops her hand
her face has the cold, smoldering light
of distant stars. Fallen into a world
of tropic snow, each ground patch manned
with pitying looks, store fronts—she's pulled
into herself like one whose fight

has gone. In the children's tale,
the star god throws her daughter from the sky
for being mulish and ungrateful,
and dooms her to wander here—a pale
un-worded stranger. The gate
to home slowly dissolves. Her eyes

will only settle where bare space
has been, and though the people try
to ease her, there's no serum
for her plight. She's scared in this place,
missing a wildness she is far from.
Her skin burns and she cannot cry.

Swan Children

The yard is quiet in the day, and when the vespers call
us to return indoors, my husband loiters

by the lakeshore as a ghost would, searching for them. I did not mean
that they should leave us long. But when the rain

pelted the flagstone, the youngest, petulant, clawed in fever,
screamed the name of her mother (just two months buried); the other

clutching my skirts, white knuckled, his pockmarks ready to bloom
or just scabbed over, feared the pasture fox, the storm,

ravens—the caw, he said, threatened to take him—that picked
the heads of rotting, frostbitten cabbage. Bitter, slow

as the first light, as the fox slipping the light latch of the coop, I stole
them out of sleep. Specter-like and inconsolable,

they still haunt our water, my husband thinking the pair lovelier
than any he has seen—and though they move

as solemnly as ships, their arching necks erect, I see
them dimming with each shortened day. It's me

they couldn't anchor in, their small hands grabbing in despair
like those who cannot float, and drown. I steered

their need out of our house, and saw their nightgowned bodies drop
from the step, the green slope, the dock. They trusted, reckoned

my coldness was a mother's they could tame as chicks would take
to the air with wet feathers, their wings part-formed. Dark hair

clumped slowly into tufts of down—a nightmare swim
turned to a waterlogged eternity. It's their sea-home

that expects them now, and soon, on a cold morning, I will go out,
the season colorless, the grass blighted and hard, and know

at last the loneliness that holds them to this place, the song
emptied of grace, that cannot make a sound.

The Edge of the World

Throughout the Middle Ages from Gildas to Gerald, the occupants of Britain believed the British Isles to be located at the edge of civilization, a last, lonely outpost before the "uncrossable" sea.

    –Asa Simon Mittman, *Maps and Monsters in Medieval England*

Here, there are no sirens, and the singing
        grass breaks off
in winds that never stop. My head is ringing
        from the bluff's

sharp drop, and I can see you shrinking back,
        already small
behind the granite rocks, the seaweed's black
        and brittle wall

parched to the sand. It's either stay or swim
        the endless deep,
and you've gone after heron nests in limbs
        too high to leap

into. I'd fall behind you in a second
        if I could,
but all around me there's just salt that beckons,
        water, wood.

Instruct a body how to pike and dive
      from cliff to sea,
and there, murk-netted in undertow, I'll give
      both you and me

up to the elements. The heron trees
      circled by hawks,
dusk skulking close, I trace the goose flesh on your knees
      down to your socks,

damp as the sand, cold as the red moon
      swelling above
this sky of water, wrecked with ships strewn
      storm and timber from their loves.

Tattoo

I was left alone
seeking the visible world.

     –William Wordsworth, *The Prelude*

In the months before your father's death, you started to want
     signs that you never had, to feel
the pigment rush into your skin, to know by touch
     what you could still not name, by blood.
For hours, you scoured pieces inscribed on stranger's wrists,
     their arms, into pale ribs, the bony arch
of an instep. Each of these images strained to remember
     something lost—an ex or a childhood
wish, a grudge that can no longer be forgiven—
     a way to show that where the shade
had been, glare seeped, a way of drawing grief
     close, keeping it visible.
I knew even before that where he went, a part
     of you went too, its absence stark
as the unmarked patch under your shoulder—an empty space
     for which you could not find a shape,
that I still see at night left naked by the sheet—indelible,
     this little sleep that takes us.

Prodigal

Even your distance had been far from us—
        Eugene then Uruguay, your girlfriend's house, a van
                or camping plot, three-month rehab in Vermont.

And I, in turn, grew used to distancing, sensing
        your bloodshot eyes across
                our high school parking lot, turning away.

Resenting all you took—the gold-plated, pendant
        star that outlived Dachau, the totaled car
                and crashed-in tree, hours on the telephone we lost

to you: marooned Thanksgiving in New York, in need
        of money, cigarettes, bupropion, rides to your restaurant job, the clinic,
                school, home from L.A.—needing

new clothes, replacement strings for those you broke
        on your guitar. I avoided you, even before
                you left, begrudging always your sad ballads

and sleep-squandered hours—I thought your gloom
        a surefire death. And here and there a song request, a letter,
                shirts for your birthday and a story about the snow

for your small daughter whom I barely know,
        but whom I'm certain our father suffers for, grieving
                each morning for her foreignness—an ache that he can't touch.

Though you would bleed him dry. Though you'd return
      some far-off April to the home he could not fortify, where
            he would laugh and hand to you each ragged peony and stone—

the house floors gouged with burn marks, palimpsests of scuffs:
      that he'd give to you, brother, if he could, all that I hoard
            in greed, in fear—this house still begging your forgiveness.

V

"Self-portrait as the Allegory of Painting"

Artemisia Gentileschi, 1638-1639

To say that painting is a woman, buxom
and green clad, neck in shade—that she
is hunched and square faced, graced
with large, muscular hands, thick wristed,
her massive, tilting figure set
back in a corner, dimly lit, her narrow brush
pointed above the picture we can't see—

to say her art's hulking and awkward, flawed
from stiffened bristles, umber-caked
palette knives, poor light—that it lacks
daintiness or fine lines, shapes idealized,
gossamer draped or chaise reclined—
that it favors instead the full dark brows
and unkempt head, grim skies, back rooms, straw beds—

to say I've lied to you, claiming I've learned
distrust of symbols, scales shrunken
to fit, glares tempered by ornate frames,
angles widened and rounded out,
those foregrounds prop-ridden and fixed
as parquet floors, as marble steps worn
smooth by jet-lagged crowds, anxious

minutes shaken off like snow fallen
on dry sleeves, champagne held to the lips
but never drunk. There is a restlessness
I've found, a company that's stuck
in cool dark rooms and galleries,
in the taffeta-pressed torso
of her likeness, bent, strong boned, plain dressed—

to say I've loved you even in artifice—
museums' preservation glass, the brush
or months-dry page, the dust-rimmed heft
of a keepsake box—its cypress distance ticking
at my view just as you start in me, just as I summon
snow-deep mornings we strung maple trees with tin pails,
dipping our fingers in them, tasting the spring.

Purple Finches

When the kids flooded our school each fall, lugging
their trunks crammed full of necessaries—UGG boots
and Nas CDs, pralines the mothers baked
the day before they'd pass into our charge
their teenage girls, their sons—the maples blazed

in the September sky, winter's thin fingers tugging
our scarves and hems, the sun's paling salute
each evening earlier and more cold. The year ahead
loomed large as Bear Hill leaning towards the clouds
that forecasted flu and late-night calls, your favorites

busted for cigarettes or booze or sex, sent
home—our fence invisible in white drifts,
the classroom's jittery pull of stretched hands
eager to name the *treachery,* the *duke,*
Miranda's small, chaste isolation.

And through the months, students had brought me things:
a Dalian map still on my desk, a pilsner glass,
a coral necklace (bought in Mexico
one spring break), porcelain bird whistles
from Shanghai, a blue Murano paperweight.

May sprouted daffodils, the soccer fields
squelching and lush and checked with puddles,
when we donned our robes, watching the seniors
fling their hats before their families drove
them home. Scattered with Solo cups and lost tassels,

the school lawns hushed. We left the scraps out
for raccoons, skunks, the birds whose cast-off nests
I would discover every fall: woven with kite string
and our Shetland's mane, the soft hairs
of our last white dog, the trapped damp of the rain.

"Girl Worker at the Ponemah Mills, Taftsville, CT"

Jack Delano, 1940

In one version of the story, she is the girl
    who struck from home, the first to leave
her father's farm for the tenement-rowed miles
    of a start-up town, to doff her childhood

rooms for dormitory beds, the churn
    of millrace water—for fingers that burned
in sleep from the pull of the loom. But here, we see
    her left alone. Centered behind

white lines of spools, her downturned focus mines
    the spinning mule's drone for something
out of reach. This picture documents
    her rapt concentration in the mapped

directives of an act from which she's set apart:
    the bobbin-whir reeling its seams,
her role unseen. Hers is the work of puppeteer
    and doll. Hers is the hand masked

by the one holding the strings. And in this version
    she is small, a cog undone
in the machine—though if I turn
    to look again, she reappears

as the white spider in the leaves,
      half hidden by the shade, who casts
her line and dangles patiently, biding
      her time, counting the threads she weaves.

Still Life

Having mastered the depiction of real objects, postures, or aspects of the natural world, the artist progressed to the realm of imagination and invention.

    –Claudia Swan, *Art, Science and Witchcraft in Early Modern Holland*

I. *Ad Vivum*

It's difficult to give back life
to what's been cut off from the living:
spirea leaves curling in heat,
the red-clipped grapes spilling
out of their silver bowl, a bright
tail feather that's been shed from flight,
cast from the air to the slope of a roof.

I search these remnants for proof
they once belonged to other bodies,
noting the bristles on each stem,
the fine, vineyard-lane film dulling
the fruit, the rounded point where the quill
buried itself in the flesh of the bird.
Of course, the setup is unnatural.

A dusk-hour bloom will settle on it all,
and what the viewer's meant to take
away is not the demarcation
between what lives and what does not,
rather how well the painter tricks
her into thinking that this version
fits the world and gives it back.

II. *Uyt Den Gheest*

Paint what you see. The bridal veil
cascades its whiteness on the lawn
beside the house where I grew up,
where gravel crunched at each approach,
and snowdrifts waited till late March
when at last the mountain winds would stop.
But now, in front of me, the petals
sharpen and announce their separate
botanic forms: square edged, definite.
Lovely alone, lovely to show
in each exacting stroke, to know
I've rendered cleanly what the heart
always refashions out of scale.
But still I have to choose which truth
to tell, and so decide to call
the flower *spirea,* that I'll be faithful
to the image shaping on the page
where the vineyard has outgrown the old stone
wall and the swallows dip and plane in the sun.

Apology

After this long, and after everything,
the ladybugs have reappeared: their shells
in clusters on the sills and up-facing wells
of lamps, the arm of the chair. Remembering,

I see you ducked in the low ceiling of your room,
one tired hand propped on your cheek, one cross-checking
cadences for rifts—new snow flecking
the pavement just outside the door where gloom

skulked on the curb, hunched in an overcoat,
always awaiting us. And now, in my first year
of marriage, I watch our winter outcasts near
somehow to reclamation in the crude throat

of this residence, where pardon crawls
like light across my arm, then settles back into the walls.

The Painter and the Color-blind

To see you more, I break your bleached-white locks
into five shades of fair. The surf crashes
on sun-baked rocks, and from the campers' fires, ash
floats and settles on the docks

like early snow. I point at clouds that blush
and trap the sun, begging your view,
Isn't it nice? You nod, and in the sky, two
gulls steady themselves against the current's rush.

The composition's this: me, you, the drift
of crisp air into cold. Fall light. Moonlight.
The blaze of snow I never can get right
except to watch its steady falling shift

our bright room into dusk. You ask what color
the sea is—your eyes, brackish green, not possible
to name—so I try *emerald,* less and less able
to explain, to part the deeper swell from *foam* or

metal gray, slate blue. Winter arrives, sweeps
piles of russet beech leaves to our door.
I help you choose a tie, and more and more
each strange encounter settles us, keeps

innocent the way we both pretend
to see the same world caught in a spark
of firelight; the fast and splintering dark
whose shades we only separately attend.

Hudson River School

Nearing the Tappan Zee, it's close to dusk, though I can see
the outcrop's pale colossus loom above the water, larger
than I could have dreamt—the bluffs, the river, here so wide
it takes me minutes, vision-struck, to cross. I'd found the artists' scenes

hard to believe, thinking them glorified—the hills too grand, the distance
hung above the small, dark shapes of men, of deer, its luminescent weight
that of the moon swelling to fill an upstairs window. I thought
the palette was too pure: all white-gold rock and olive green, no bristly plants

or undergrowth, no mud, the sky always cerulean. So I shied
from their landscapes early on, seeking instead the clefts of portrait
flesh, the drift of lilies half formed on a pond, only to find,
on my way back to some cold city, what I'd always missed—

the steel bridge launching an arc from ledge to cliff, the sun's glare
in my eyes almost enough to mask what's really there.

Pravda

Russian: "Truth"

I. *Fortune-teller's House, Baltimore*

She's read the palms of nearly everyone.
Days float. Smoke eddies filter evening sun

and fall around her, cloaking her wooden chair,
the glass-top table where her clients dare

to peek at what's been written in their skin.
For her, the future has already been

visited and left behind—the young bride spinning
in rain, a house in flames—she's learned to thin

her certainties with *maybe, someday, if.*
She knows that longing, at its root, is stiff

as December's ice-bound roses, that it demands
the tangible, and so she cradles in her hands

each upturned wrist, studies the threads
that show the bearing of the heart, the head.

II. *Frederick Smith Gymnasium, New Hampton, New Hampshire*

Ballplayers are the sound of rubber tumbling
over wood, squeaking on lacquer, the thud
and leather smack of a pass. The bleachers shudder
at threes, the crowd's breath resting on limbs
crouching and flexed, stretching before they climb
the air's hot press, leaving the other bodies
floor-bound, necks strained up. The fans study
formation, placement, plays. But in this game,

the driving mind wins over muscle, and chance
seizes when it can. I see at once
the way a win eludes all bets, pends
in the seconds ticking down, the shot's
unlikely arc, boards where the coaches plot
arrows and x's, picks, possible ends.

III. *Mariinsky Theater, St. Petersburg*

All day, we walk by the embankments.
I am lost. A new friend guides me by
the massive buildings, past the chilly flanks

of river swelling alongside us. The sky
is dawn colored all day, and every girl
we pass staggers and flits, my jet-lagged eyes

taking their speed for grace, the slight curl
of fingers for the fledging of a swan.
Like hard, stone-channeled water, memories purl

against this foreign backdrop and are gone:
my first ballet—in winter velvet—peering
from the balcony, the soloist not lonely

as she leapt across the stage (sheer
light); the way my mother always wished
that I had stayed with dance; the spotlight trance steering

a body when the mind forgets; pliés
held low to the floor; the barre; a plain
stance practiced in sequence, minutes, days.

Some learning's penned into the tendon, bone.
Here, Russian vowels retract like proper
laughter, recede like late snows. Like the April sun

this theater removes its mask, and I remember
how the story ends (a broken heart,
a dive), remember how, retired, the Kirov dancer

held her body like a bird's—her art
drawn in her neck, her out-turned toes, her shoulders
when she once stopped our class to tell her secret:

how the ballerinas used to stuff their
pointe shoes with the "truth," propping their weight
on scraps they tore out of the paper.

Philomela

At first there was no sound, only the needle's dart
and prick, a minnow in and out
of pondweed holes, finally surfacing in light.

But here, always the one small shuttered window caves
to what's outside—the orange grove,
sun cutting the mourning dove's

low coo, the evening grinding at last to lull
the throbbing head and wrists, spools
everywhere unraveling her half-stitched tale.

And still the stone tower crumbles. And still night lifts
her swollen fingers to the cleft
of nothingness waiting outside these walls. Only the soft-

fledged trilling sticks, is stifled inside her like a moan.
Her throat's song finally spun—
and in the leaves, the wrens

were cheeping *twilight, twilight,* and were gone.